every 100 turtle doves there were 40 years ago there are now only nine.

Published by Red Herring Publishing
© Ann Lamb & Demelza Craven 2018
No illustrations may be reproduced without the permission of the artist

ISBN 978-1-9997839-2-1

printed by Colour Print, Norfolk

When Turtle Doves Fly

written by Demelza Craven & designed by Ann Lamb
for all of the artists involved in the creation of this book see pages 34-35

Dedication

To all those who have given their time and hearts to the cause of the turtle dove.

'If I had a flower for every time I thought of you
I could walk in my garden forever'

Alfred Lord Tennyson

... and pomegranates aching with ruby-bright flesh.

Contents

Two Turtle Doves

We're all familiar with the 'two turtle doves' from the Christmas Carol, but what of their real counterparts? At Christmas time turtle doves actually are a very long way from England living in the semi-arid scrubland of Mali.

*Turtle doves are in trouble, they have suffered a population decline of over 90% in their UK breeding grounds since 1995 and a decline of 78% across Europe since 1980.

Every year turtle doves take the perilous journey from the UK to Mali in the autumn and then back again in the spring. They weigh only 140g and yet their migration flight is a round trip of more than 11,000 km.

Using satellite tracking, the 'Operation Turtle Dove' team have discovered much useful information about the turtle doves' migration route. This insight into what the doves face and what their needs and requirements are is helping to formulate a recovery strategy for turtle doves.

We would like to share with you our imagined turtle dove migration, which gives a little snapshot in time as our turtle dove passes through various countries, landscapes and situations, whilst everyday life goes on.

We have also put together some useful information on how we can all help turtle doves simply by growing their food plants, providing water and enhancing habitats. Currently the Turtle Dove is the UK's fastest declining species of bird, it would be wonderful if we could reverse this trend.

Ann Lamb

*Turtle doves are Red listed on the UKs 'Birds of Conservation Concern 4' (Eaton et al. 2015) and have been assessed as 'Vulnerable' to extinction in Europe on the IUCN Red List of Threatened Species 2017.

England, *turr turr*

It was on a night, not so different from this one, that the turtle dove flew. A night when the feathery seed heads of the traveller's joy had no kernels left to bear and the honeysuckle had breathed its last perfumed breath. It was a night when the moonlight dappled through the hedgerows and the air became cold and still. It was then that the turtle dove *turred* her last in the English hedgerow. She ruffled her lacy feathers, rolled a golden eye skywards, and took flight…

She spread her wings wide and glided over the isle she called home. Past the hamlet where carollers would hark *'two turtle doves'* in her frost-ridden absence. Past the glow of the jeweller's shop window with its golden doves for constancy. She did not notice the bookshop with its old edition of *'The Phoenix and the Turtle'* quilled long ago in the time of ruffs and parchment paper. And when she rested a while on the old church spire she did not ponder upon the stained glass saint shining with her likeness. Instead she swept past them all, destined for a journey far the more ancient than bards or carol singers…

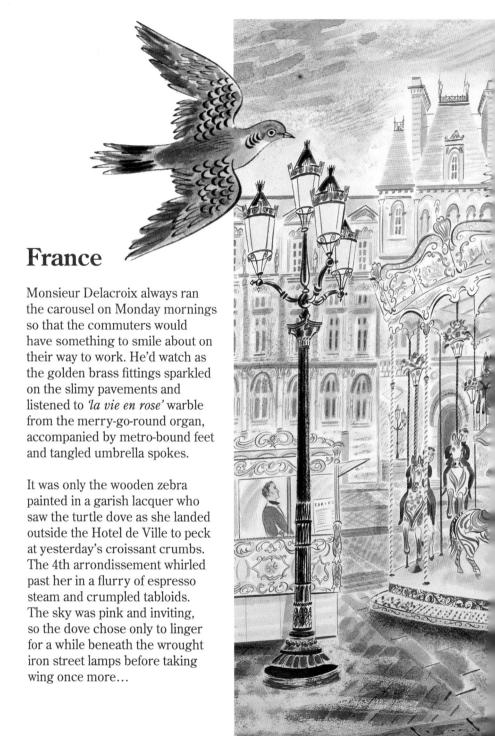

France

Monsieur Delacroix always ran the carousel on Monday mornings so that the commuters would have something to smile about on their way to work. He'd watch as the golden brass fittings sparkled on the slimy pavements and listened to *'la vie en rose'* warble from the merry-go-round organ, accompanied by metro-bound feet and tangled umbrella spokes.

It was only the wooden zebra painted in a garish lacquer who saw the turtle dove as she landed outside the Hotel de Ville to peck at yesterday's croissant crumbs. The 4th arrondissement whirled past her in a flurry of espresso steam and crumpled tabloids. The sky was pink and inviting, so the dove chose only to linger for a while beneath the wrought iron street lamps before taking wing once more…

11

Spain

The turtle dove did not consider how far she'd come by the time she reached the Mediterranean. She did not dwell on the sea she'd crossed or the fields she'd passed. Instead she flew through the olive groves, where the scent of ripening lemons lingered heady upon the air. She watched from her place beside the sun-swollen oranges, as Adriana with a penknife in one hand and a prickly pear in the other, skinned the fruit whole in a single motion. The table was laid with the fruits of the orchard, with wine which had been trodden between local toes, and buttery avocados and pomegranates arching with ruby-bright flesh.

The doves gathered upon the branches and watched as mouths were filled and faces smiled and guns were polished before the evening's dove shoot. When they left that earthy coastline, with its rosemary-scented streets, there were not so many birds as there once had been…

there were not so many birds as there once had been…

Hannah

The Pillars of Hercules & the Sea

Long shadows were cast across craggy grey rocks as the sun set upon the Pillars of Hercules.

The
turtle dove
perched upon
one Pillar in the
Mediterranean
where she could
see in the distance
the other resting on
the shoreline of North
Africa, between them
a great gulf of slowly
darkening ocean.
Here the air was
fresh on the salty
breath of the sea and the
smell of teak oil and rope
fibres carried from distant
harbours. These pillars of
rock were said to be held up
by Hercules himself, in the time
of snake-haired gorgons and
Mount Olympus. The same time
when the Goddess Fides, the
symbol of trust and good faith,
kept a turtle dove by her side
for the example they set of
true love and constancy.

...and then there was sea. Over its great expanse she flew.

Sea behind her. Sea beneath her. Sea before her.

In the obsidian blackness she could barely make out where the water ended and the sky began, the reflection of stars in water cloaking her in an orb of night. Out there it did not do to dwell on the heavy wings that bore her onwards, for who would notice if she grew weary and sank into the shadowy deep?

15

◆ Morocco ◆

In a couscous-coloured street where the smell of
sun-ripened apricots hung heavy on the air, the
turtle dove rested by a fountain. It was decorated
in zellige tiles, yellow as the sun and blue as the
sky. Their arabesque patterns followed the same
swell and fall as her feathers. She lingered on a
nearby branch and watched as Turkish slippers
avoided discarded date stones, sucked of their flesh.
She sipped at the fountain water, reserved for the
ablution rituals when the mosques sing out the
time for prayer.

Cardamon and rosewater wafted from a nearby stall
where children gathered to marvel at the oozing
honey and gems of pistachio peeking out from
beneath layers of golden baklava. As she flew from
her perch a stall keeper called Karim wondered 'if
the depiction of man and beast is forbidden then are
the patterns in the tiles inspired by those glorious
wings? Or their colours based on those sky blue
necks?' But he soon forgot his thoughts and she
flew on over the busy streets, above the cages of
sorrowful birds and above the bowls of cumin and
bartering hands.

Western Sahara

When the dove reached Western Sahara she took shelter
from a sand storm. The restless dunes surrounded her and as they
did they told stories. Stories of Bedouin tribesmen painted on old
cave walls. They whispered of the native hounds, the ones th
called *'el hor'* meaning *'noble one'*, and they sang a
song of fleeing gazelle whose pounding hoov
could be heard to sound the very same a
the torrents of oscillating sand.

The spiralling dust told the secrets of the desert until there were none left to exhale and the dove could fly on through the rose-gold darkness, beneath the light of the fading stars.

19

Mauritania

When at last she reached Mauritania there was no water to be found. Just mile upon mile of arid desert.

Anan's robes were cloying and his legs were heavy and the movement of the great camel beneath him rocked him into a leaden slumber. The bells and tassels of the herd which followed swung and chimed with their cumbersome movements. Fortunately, Anan's camel knew the journey well and she led the herd around the *'Guelb er Richat'*, the place which is known as the *'Eye of the Sahara'*. It is an eerie pool of blue in a landscape of dust and mud, and no water can be found in its structure.

A single feather fell unseen into its blue abyss as the turtle doves passed overhead...

y flew on past Nouakchott where the sound of recited poetry told of stories so old no one had ever thought to write them down. The dove did not stay to listen as her kind had flown past for years enough to remember since before the tales were told.

Senegal

When the turtle dove reached Senegal, she was just
in time to see Abdala haul the Atlantic bonito
shimmering from the water.

Here, the sea lapped
at a shoreline of white sand
and pointed palm leaves. But the turtle dove did
not marvel at the silvery scales of the newly-
netted catch, nor did she linger at the languid scent of
mangos mellowing upon the branch. On the beach, Agata drank
the milk of a coconut which in her language of Wolof meant *'happiness'*;
she broke the succulent shards from the shell and savoured the sweetness,
but the dove did not watch, there could be no coconut for her. Instead, she soared
over a patchwork of tropical beaches, deserts and lush rain forest, a dying sun
bathing the landscape in molten gold.
Views were something that she rarely admired,
and least of all with so many behind her.

23

Mali

It was on a night, not so different
from this one, that the turtle dove flew.
A night when the baobab fruit hung heavy from the
branches of The Tree of Life and the heat of the
earth rose and cooled in the mud-cloth darkness.
The moonlight dappled through the acacia leaves
and a tiny turtle dove landed, unseen, upon its
branches, her feathers quivering where they lay
neatly above her heart. It was then that the turtle
dove *turred* once more in the African bush, five and a
half thousand kilometres from a honeysuckle she called
home. She ruffled her lacy feathers, rolled a golden eye
skywards, and at long last rested.

She was finally in Mali, a country whose name means *'the place
where the king lives'*, a country whose main trade is in gold and
where Timbuktu is the capital city. She had survived natural predators
and the elements, a lack of food and a lack of habitat, she'd survived the
huntsmen's guns and the trappers' snares, she had not been caged and
she had not been stuffed and her tiny exhausted body had not been eaten
as a delicacy. For now she was safe, and as she brooded upon the branch,
a distant and familiar *turr* trilled through the leaves as a pair of wings beat
down beside her. It was the one who always found her in the spring, with
the scent of rosehips still lingering in his feathers. And so together at last
in Mali, they rested with their necks entwined, and dreamt a dream of
traveller's joy and fumitory flowers, of winding vetch and fields of
cloud-coloured clovers.

We will all sing *'two turtle doves'* in their absence this winter, but we can
only hope that in the spring two turtle doves still return.

honeysuckle called home...

England to Mali = 11,000 km migration flight

a journey far the more ancient than bards or carol singers...

Love, Hope & Good Faith

A trip to the library and a flick through the leaves of fiction from ancient times to now will reveal a cultural reference which appears again and again. The turtle dove flies through the pages of Shakespeare, the Bible and Arthurian legend. It is used as a symbol of trust, of constancy, of beauty and of love. They are the herald of spring, the sound of summer, the gift of *'my true love'* at Christmas time. They can be found depicted in stained glass windows, in jewellery shops and in art galleries up and down the country. And yet scientists calculate that this golden bird, once so revered, faces the possibility of complete UK extinction as a breeding species.

The decline of the turtle dove has been steep and shocking with populations falling between 1995 and 2014 by 93%. There are now just nine turtle doves for every 100 that used to thrive in the English countryside 40 years ago.

There are multiple reasons for their decline, from dove shooting in the Mediterranean to the many diseases which wild birds can fall foul of. But most shockingly of all, it is the lack of habitat and food in the UK which is likely to have had the most detrimental effect of them all.

if every person set aside an area in their garden to nurture the wild flowers which turtle doves depend upon...

We believe this is both shameful and hopeful...

...We might have all had our own part to play in their decline, but we all have the power to play a part in their return too.

Intensive farming methods have poisoned large swathes of native wild flowers which are the sole food source of the turtle dove. And a culture of *'neat tidy gardens'* and large amounts of tarmac has meant their food source is scarcer still.

But if every person set aside an area in their garden to nurture the wild flowers which turtle doves depend upon, then over the expanse of gardens, local parks, public playing fields and school grounds there could be a great nature reserve of the perfect habitat with each of us owning a little patch of it in our own outdoor spaces. By creating these habitats, we'd not only be aiding the plight of the turtle dove but a whole manner of other native wildlife which has been hit by the sanitisation of our countryside.

Hedgerows are of equally high importance, with turtle doves needing thick healthy hedgerows to nest in. Could your fence be exchanged for a hedge of native hedgerow species? Or could you encourage your local farmer to take up

an appropriate Countryside Stewardship Scheme for field borders and hedgerow care? Could you ask your local council to have a wild flower patch in your local park? Or could you encourage your local schools to get children in touch with nature by planting their own wild flower areas? There is so much that can be done to practically help this iconic bird who has shaped the cultural fabric of our country.

The turtle dove has been a symbol of hope for mankind for millennia. And now it is vital that mankind be a symbol of hope for the turtle dove. What a great shame it would be to visit a library full of books which celebrate the turtle dove as a symbol of love, hope and good faith, which has disappeared for the lack of ourselves having any love, hope or good faith to offer in return.

birdsfoot trefoil

honey suckle

bramble

dog rose

travelers joy

black medic

common vetch

red clover

Turtle Dove Garden

Turtle doves need our help; we can grow seeds, provide water and cultivate nesting sites.

Turtle doves only eat seeds (obligate granivores) and when they arrive back from migration it's really important that there are plenty of seeds available for them.

Turtle doves eat the seeds from fumitory, black medic, red and white clover, common vetch, birdsfoot trefoil, and scarlet pimpernel. Sowing a mix of seeds of these plants in the autumn will allow them to grow, flower and have seeds ready for the turtle doves to eat when they return from migration at the end of April.

Growing seeds

Seedbed: fork over the soil, remove unwanted grass and weeds, then rake to create a fine tilth, (you can use a black mulch sheet to suppress grass and weeds before preparing your seedbed).

Sowing: sprinkle or broadcast the seed over your prepared seedbed, (you can mix the seed with a little sand or compost to see more easily where it goes), firm down the soil and seeds by rolling or treading with your feet.

'Thus after the winter the spring will come, with its flowers, and you will hear the voice of the turtle dove in this land.'

Paul of the Cross

You can also grow the seeds in pots for planting out or in containers, they'd look attractive on a patio!

Water

Provide clean water in a wide shallow container or birdbath. Water is vital for turtle doves because they feed their young 'crop milk', a mix of water and seeds.

Nest sites

Turtle doves prefer to nest in high wide hedges interlaced with climbing plants like traveller's joy (wild clematis), honeysuckle, dogrose and bramble. If you have a hedge that backs onto a field let it grow as tall and wide as possible and encourage or plant with wild climbers.

Suppliers of wildflower seeds and plug plants can be found with a bit of an internet search and once you have the plants established in your garden they will self seed and you can save seeds yourself to use time and time again.

www.operationturtledove.org

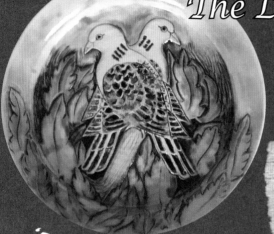

'....too lovely a creature for me to destroy.' *The Dovekeepers, by Alice Hoffn*

'*Two turtle doves & a partridge in a pear tree.*'

'For behold, the winter is past;
the rain is over and gone.
The flowers appear on
the earth, the time of
singing has come,
and the voice
of the turtle
dove is heard in
our land.'

Song of Solomon

'Now don't you see a little
turtle dove
Sitting under a mulberry tree?
See how she doth mourn her
true love,
As I shall mourn for thee,'

Folk song

'When the soul, like the
solitary turtle dove, retires
and recollects itself in
meditation to converse with
God, then the flowers,
that is, good desires, appear'.

Alphonsus Liguori

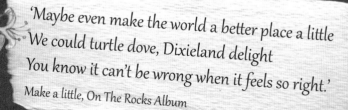

'Maybe even make the world a better place a little
We could turtle dove, Dixieland delight
You know it can't be wrong when it feels so right.'

Make a little, On The Rocks Album

'THE DAYLIGHT WAS STILL GREY, BUT KYOT IMMEDIATELY RECOGNISED THE COAT OF ARMS OF THE GRAIL ON THE TROOPS, -THEY WERE MARKED WITH TURTLE DOVES.'

'Wolfram's Parizival

'The turtle dove when widowed, lives for ever after alone in memory of her first love, and will not turn to another. So will [the author] behave to the memory of his lady.'

From the Bestiaire d'Amour

'From the molten
golden notes,
And all in tune
What a liquid ditty floats
To the turtle dove that listens
while she gloats
On the moon!'

Edgar Allen Poe

'Yea, the stork in the heavens knows her appointed times; and the turtle dove and the crane and the swallow observe the time of their coming.'

Jeremiah 8:7
King James edition

'But come; our dance,
I pray,
Your hand, my Perdita:
so turtles pair
That never mean to part.'

Shakespeare

'In order to nourish the soul you must become a turtle dove.'

Maria Maddalena De' Pazzi

33

The Artists

Ann Lamb, Graphic Designer and Jeweller: lives in a red-brick farmhouse in Thurne, with a garden which stretches all the way down to the river. She has been a passionate nature lover all of her life and considers herself very lucky to be able to see the likes of otters, cranes and bitterns from the back of her garden. She keeps bees, a thriving vegetable patch and two donkeys called Ruben and Eve. Two turtle doves used to visit her garden… And then they stopped.

Demelza, Author: lives in Catfield with a saluki called Ra.
She thinks the best way to find inspiration and see nature is from the back of a horse, - which is where she will frequently be found. When she's not cantering she's writing stories for her Literary Agent. Her hobbies include sketching, long country walks and drinking too much Darjeeling tea! Demelza has never seen a turtle dove.

Both Demelza and Ann keep wild areas in their gardens and really hope that this book might inspire you to do the same.

This book could not have happened without the generosity of the following artists who gave their art in aid of turtle doves.

front cover
Vanessa Lubach

page 5
Sue Farrow-Jones

end papers
Ann Lamb

page 6
Catherine Rowe

page 3
Robert Gillmor

page 8
Tricia Newell